Removing the Roadblocks to Health & Healing

by Annette Capps

Unless otherwise indicated, all Scripture quotations are taken from the King James Version KJV of the Bible.

19 18 17   6 5 4 3 2 1

Removing the Roadblocks to Health and Healing
ISBN 13: 978-1-937578-58-9

First Printing

Removing the Roadblocks to Health and Healing

The Bible establishes the fact that Jesus Christ came to restore us to right relationship with God. Through His blood, we are free from sin. By His stripes, we are healed. This sacrifice was without limitation to every person, yet not all are free from sin and not all are healed and well. Why? Because it requires something of each individual person.

But as many as received him, to them gave he power to become the sons of God, even to them that believe on his name:

John 1:12

In order to be free from sin, you must receive Him as your Lord and Savior and believe. To be healed and live in health, it is necessary to *receive Him as your Great Physician* and *believe* that He bore your

1

sickness and pain. *Receive* and believe. It is accomplished and in God's book, it is done! All debts are paid, healing and health is credited to your account. God is not the problem. We sometimes cause our own problems by hindering the manifestation of the health that God has given us.

Let's examine some of these "roadblocks" to health and healing:

1. Claiming Sickness as Belonging to You

Has anyone ever asked you what kind of car you drive? Your answer usually goes like this, "I have a blue Chevy Malibu." I *have*. I *have* signifies something you possess that belongs to you. You claimed the car as your own. Now if you were driving your sister's car that you borrowed for the day, you would reply, "I am driving my sister's white Ford Escort." You are agreeing you are driving the car for the day, but deny that it belongs to you. Sickness is an energy that might try to attach itself to you, but DO NOT CLAIM IT or accept it as yours. When you say:

"I have arthritis," you are acknowledging that it belongs to you.

"My high blood pressure," it is yours.

"I am sick," you are what you say you are.

So what do I say then? How do I talk to my spouse, my doctor etc?

"My knee has been hurting" or "It hurts here," acknowledges *what is*, but does not establish ownership.

"I am currently experiencing these symptoms_____," describes what is *happening now* but it is *subject to change*.

"I feel dizzy," tells what your body is feeling, but it does not commit you to being dizzy for the rest of your life.

These are better ways to say what needs to be said, and you should only say them when necessary. Rather than continually repeat these words and focus on them, focus on the

3

end result—health—whether health comes miraculously, through doctors, medicine, holistic treatments, or change of diet; it does not matter how God helps you enter into divine health.

Now I know that you understand the power of words, but some of you may say that this is only a matter of semantics. No, it is a matter of what you say affecting your body. It is a matter of making a passing pain into a condition, a temporary illness into a syndrome, and sometimes into a terminal condition. You do not deny what you are experiencing, but you call for the end result which is health. By your words and beliefs, you can make a temporary condition temporary, or solidify it into a concrete permanent illness.

For we all stumble in many things. If anyone does not stumble in word, he is a perfect man, able also to bridle the whole body.

Indeed, we put bits in horses' mouths that they may obey us, and we turn their whole body. James 3:2-3 NKJV

4

If you can control your words, you can control your whole body. The Amplified translation says, "…able to control his whole body and to curb his entire nature." James also says that the words you speak can even *defile* your body:

And the tongue is a fire, a world of iniquity. The tongue is so set among our members that it defiles the whole body, and sets on fire the course of nature; and it is set on fire by hell. James 3:6 NKJV

The Amplified version says, "…contaminating and depraving the whole body and setting on fire the wheel of birth — the cycle of man's nature…"

If you can defile and make your body sick by your words, how much more can you make yourself well by speaking words of health?

"THANK YOU LORD MY BODY RESPONDS TO THE WORDS OF MY MOUTH AND I AM WELL AND MY BODY IS WELL. THE SAME SPIRIT THAT

RAISED CHRIST FROM THE DEAD NOW QUICKENS AND MAKES ALIVE EVERY CELL IN MY BODY!"

2. Belief in Tribal DNA

I believe from my research that the scriptures above referring to the "course of nature" or the "wheel of birth" relate to what you have inherited, your DNA. You may have inherited a great DNA from your family genes. Your family goes back generations and so I refer to it as "tribal DNA." Nature has given you a gift of a healthy set of genes. James says that you can destroy that wonderful gift by your tongue. The words you speak can bring sickness as well as health.

Maybe your family has had a lot of sickness and so you say, "Well, my Dad died at an early age of _____(fill in the blank, heart attack, diabetes, stroke) and I'll probably die early too."

Your DNA is not the determining factor of your health. You are. Yes, you may have inherited some genes that have a tendency to produce certain illnesses, but what you *say*, what you *believe*, and *how you take care of yourself* will determine the outcome. If you choose to believe that you are a victim of your DNA, it will be a self fulfilling prophecy. The key is, YOU HAVE A CHOICE!

You just read the scriptures above and James says that by your words, you can change "the wheel of birth" for good or for bad. In your situation, I would declare loudly (in private):

"I WILL NOT INHERIT SICKNESS, DISEASE, OR MALFUNCTION OF ANY KIND BECAUSE I AM A CHILD OF GOD, BORN OF HIS SPIRIT, AND MY INHERITANCE IS FROM GOD MY FATHER! LIFE MORE ABUNDANTLY!"

The physical world is created from the spiritual realm and your spiritual inheritance carries more authority than your physical inheritance. Just as the physical earth was not created in a day, your physical body may take time to respond to the spiritual input that you just unleashed by those words. Some biologists are now determining that DNA is not a sure thing in the development of disease. One thing is certain from a Biblical perspective and that is: your words affect your body and your beliefs affect your body. From a natural perspective, taking care of yourself by exercising, eating well, and seeking advice from health professionals also affects your health.

Since you have a choice of what to say and what to believe about health, wouldn't it be better to believe health is available?

Because you have the ultimate choice over your body, isn't it better to treat it like the temple where the Holy Spirit dwells?

Or do you not know that your body is the temple of the Holy Spirit who is in you, whom you have from God, and you are not your own? 1 Corinthians 6:19 NKJV

8

3. Using Infirmity as a Tool

A very big roadblock to health that no one really talks about is that sickness, illness, pain, and infirmity appear to have some big advantages from some people's point of view. I want to make you aware of this because I have dealt with some who use their "illness" as a way to get attention. Sickness or physical problems become a "tool" that can be used to:

Gain attention and sympathy

Have an excuse to not participate

Have an excuse not to work

Get special discounts or other monetary help

I had one person tell me they really wanted to be well, but what would they do if they could no longer get their disability check?

My intention in writing this is to help you find any hindrances in your life that prevent

9

you from receiving your healing and living in health. This may not apply to you, but ask yourself the question:

"Am I receiving any perks from this illness?"

There is no judgement or condemnation, just be honest. If a person chooses to receive money over health, that is simply a decision that is made. The Bible tells us in 3 John 1:2 that God wants us to *prosper and be in health*. You can have <u>both</u> — money and live in health. By meditating on this scripture, you can overcome that fear:

Beloved, I pray that you may prosper in all things and be in health, just as your soul prospers. 3 John 1:2 NKJV

If there are any other perks you receive by not being well, acknowledge it and talk to God about it. Perhaps the Holy Spirit can help you through reading the scriptures to realize that you can have the love of God and feel His Presence and this will become more comforting and satisfying than human sympathy.

Rather than using illness as an excuse to escape events you don't want to attend or participate, maybe you could be well, live in health and just say, "That is not something I want to do." The devil really tries to trip us up on the details, but it is the *"little foxes that spoil the vines."* Song of Solomon 2:15

When Jesus encountered the man at the pool of Bethesda, he had been infirm 38 years and appears to have developed a victim mentality. When Jesus asked him, "Will you be made whole?" his response was, "I have no one to help me."

And a certain man was there, which had an infirmity thirty and eight years.

When Jesus saw him lie, and knew that he had been now a long time in that case, he saith unto him, Wilt thou be made whole?

The impotent man answered him, Sir, I have no man, when the water is troubled, to put me into the pool: but while I am coming, another steppeth down before me.

Jesus saith unto him, Rise, take up thy bed, and walk.

And immediately the man was made whole, and took up his bed, and walked: and on the same day was the sabbath.

John 5:5-9

After being ill and in pain for such a length of time, it is understandable that he felt alone, abandoned and hopeless. But he had not encountered Jesus! At Jesus' command, he obeyed His Word and walked. I am sure he had no idea what he was going to do next, but it must be better than lying by the pool all day gathering sympathy!

Once you have really had an experience with the Great Physician and searched His Word, you will come to understand that He is able to provide <u>ALL</u> you have need of: emotionally, financially, and physically. He is your Great Physician and Healer.

4. Holding on to Negative Emotions

Please notice I said HOLDING ON to negative emotions. Negative emotions happen as a reaction to situations and you cannot necessarily stop your feelings nor should you. But just like the energy of sickness, you must let them pass. You can choose to experience the feeling and let go of it. If you continue to talk about it, think about it and exercise judgement against yourself and others, it will set up like concrete. In other words, you will turn that negative energy into a physical reality in your body.

There is no question that your emotions affect your health. We all know this even on a subconscious level because you hear it in our speech. Humans say things like, "I worried myself sick." "It scared him to death." "When I heard it, it just made me sick to my stomach." "She upset me so bad that I got a migraine headache."

Anger, hurt, fear, jealousy, rage, resentment. These are just some of the emotions that we all experience at some time in our lives and these have a detrimental effect not only on our mental health but our physical health as well if we are unwilling to commit them to the Lord and let them go.

Are you living in physical pain? Have you had a painful experience that you haven't been able to let go of or resolve? Is something paining you in your relationships? Your work? When I receive a letter from a partner asking me why they can't get healed of terrible pain, I ask them if they have also experienced a terrible emotional pain of some type. There seems to be a correlation between emotional and physical pain.

Isaiah 53:4 (CJB) declares: *"In fact, it was our diseases he bore, our pains from which he suffered; ..."*

All of the emotional pain you have ever suffered, every traumatic experience,

Jesus suffered and bore for you. There is no need for you to continue in emotional and physical pain, however the emotional pain must be acknowledged and released to Him.

Jeremiah 30:17 captures the essence of the love of God and His desire to restore:

For I will restore health unto thee, and I will heal thee of thy wounds, saith the Lord;

The Word of God clearly shows the relationship between our emotions and our health and encourages us to discipline and train ourselves to gain control over anger, envy, and resentment:

He who is slow to anger has great understanding, but he who is hasty of spirit exposes and exalts his folly.
A calm and undisturbed mind and heart are the life and health of the body, but envy, jealousy, and wrath are like rottenness of the bones.   Proverbs 14:29-30 AMPLIFIED

5. Refusing to Forgive

Someone once said, "Rather than asking 'What is wrong with you?', it is more accurate to ask 'Who is wrong with you?'" Getting crosswise with someone has a most unfavorable effect on health.

There is a difference in *feeling* unforgiving and *refusing* to forgive. How many times have you heard someone say, "That is unforgivable," or "I will never forgive him for that," or "I could never forgive that."? Your words become a snare when you say these sort of things. Jesus would never ask us to do something we are incapable of.

Truly I tell you, whoever says to this mountain, Be lifted up and thrown into the sea! and does not doubt at all in his heart but believes that what he says will take place, it will be done for him.

For this reason I am telling you, whatever you ask for in prayer, believe

16

(trust and be confident) that it is granted to you, and you will [get it].

And whenever you stand praying, if you have anything against anyone, forgive him and let it drop (leave it, let it go), in order that your Father Who is in heaven may also forgive you your [own] failings and shortcomings and let them drop.

Mark 11:23-25 AMPLIFIED

Here Jesus tells us some important information:

1. If you believe what you say, it will happen.

2. When you pray, have faith for what you are asking for, and it will happen.

3. While you are praying, forgive and let it go.

So if we believe what Jesus said, and we declare "I can't forgive," then you will have what you say and you will not be able to forgive. If you cannot forgive, then you might as well stop praying because that is part of this package. Now before you give up and say you just can't do it, let's take that same package and use it to do what Jesus says. Are you willing?

1. Say out loud, "I can and I will forgive in Jesus' name."

2. Pray and ask God to give you a willing and forgiving heart and have faith it is done.

3. While you are praying, say, "Lord I forgive _____ by faith in the name of Jesus."

You may not feel like doing it and you may not feel instant forgiveness, but we are not moved by what we hear, feel, or see; we are moved by the Word of God! Use your faith to forgive. Forgive on faith, not on feeling! Faith in God's Word works for forgiveness as well as finances, healing, and salvation.

6. Feeding the Spirit of Infirmity

In order to survive, an idea must have attention and be fed. It may sound strange to put it this way, but the idea of being sick or unwell can dissipate and starve if you don't feed it with your thinking, meditating and talking. If you feed the idea of wellness with your thoughts, activities and speech, health will grow and increase.

When Jesus released the woman with the spirit of infirmity, she had been bound 18 years and no doubt most of her waking thoughts were of how bad she was and what she couldn't do and how she hurt. No hope. Everyone who saw her agreed with this assessment and contributed their pity, feeding the idea of her bondage.

I believe at the moment Jesus spoke and said "Woman, thou are loosed from thine infirmity!" she was released instantly from the idea in her mind that she was permanently bowed over. She was released from that image and identity. How she saw herself changed, and hope and faith flooded her heart and mind.

And there was a woman there who for eighteen years had had an infirmity caused by a spirit (a demon of sickness). She was bent completely forward and utterly unable to straighten herself up or to look upward.

And when Jesus saw her, He called [her to Him] and said to her, Woman, you are released from your infirmity!

Then He laid [His] hands on her, and instantly she was made straight, and she recognized and thanked and praised God.

Luke 13:11-13 AMPLIFIED

This says that the sickness was caused by a spirit, but Jesus said, "You are released from your infirmity." So was it a spirit or was it an infirmity that belonged to her? I believe that a spirit attached itself to her body and she accepted it as her own. Perhaps her own mother had such a problem and she fed the idea that she would probably

20

inherit it. Demons will often follow family members until someone stops them with the mighty name of Jesus. Or, she might have been at a low spot, feeling defeated, angry and unforgiving and a spirit took advantage of her weakened condition. Then, she could see herself no other way. We are not given the information and what really matters is there is deliverance from infirmity of every kind.

Are you feeding a spirit of sickness? Do you watch television with all the bombardment of commercials suggesting drugs for every sickness and disease? Do you listen when they describe the symptoms, comparing them with your own? Do you watch medical shows, real or fiction, and become fascinated with analyzing your own health? Is searching the internet for a diagnosis of your symptoms becoming an obsession?

If yes, you are feeding a spirit of infirmity.

Is it OK if you get well without ever having a "diagnosis" or discovering what is wrong with you?

Have you ever searched the internet to try to determine why you feel so good? Have you ever made an appointment with your doctor to find out why you have so much energy?

If you focus on the good things with your health, your health is fed and becomes greater. When you *do* the things that help your health, even marginally, you are feeding a spirit of wellness.

Examine the amount of time you spend every day listening to, reading, or meditating on life, health, beauty and God's Word. Then compare it to the amount of time you are subjected to suggestions of bad health, death, destruction, and ugliness in the world. In order for health to grow strong, you must feed it with good things including gratitude and thankfulness. If you weigh these things on a scale, would you find that you are "feeding infirmity and starving health?" or are you "feeding health and starving infirmity?"

Changing the image of sickness and weakness to an image of health and strength requires daily feeding of life-giving substance and the starving of thoughts and images of sickness and death.

Finally, my brethren, be strong in the Lord, and in the power of his might.

Ephesians 6:10

I AM STRONG IN THE LORD AND MY BODY IS STRONG!

But if the Spirit of him that raised up Jesus from the dead dwell in you, he that raised up Christ from the dead shall also quicken your mortal bodies by his Spirit that dwelleth in you. Romans 8:11

THE SAME SPIRIT THAT RAISED CHRIST FROM THE DEAD DWELLS IN ME AND NOW QUICKENS AND MAKES ALIVE EVERY CELL OF MY BODY!

7. Ignoring the Leadings of the Holy Spirit and Your Spirit

In Deuteronomy 28:1-2 (NKJV), we are given the key to living in the blessings of God:

Now it shall come to pass, if you diligently obey the voice of the Lord your God, to observe carefully all His commandments which I command you today, that the Lord your God will set you high above all nations of the earth.

And all these blessings shall come upon you and overtake you, because you obey the voice of the Lord your God:

It seems we are quick to claim and declare the blessings of Abraham are ours, including health and prosperity, but these first two verses set the conditions:

1. Obey the voice of the Lord.

2. Observe His commandments.

Today, we have the Holy Spirit in us to

lead us and guide us. If we obey His voice and act upon His Word, He will lead us into the blessings and out of the cursings.

A real roadblock to healing is ignoring what you are being led to do. For instance, you may have a digestive issue and something (someone - the Holy Spirit) keeps impressing you to stop eating or drinking something you really enjoy. This is not a commandment for religious purposes, this is the Holy Spirit trying to let you know that what you are eating is causing your digestive problem! Now you have a choice...keep eating what you want and keep your stomach pain or stop. But if you continue to ignore the Holy Spirit, please don't call or write and ask why you can't get healed!

The Holy Spirit may be leading you to apologize to someone and you don't want to.

The Holy Spirit will ALWAYS lead you in line with the Word and will always lead you to forgive. If you ignore that leading, it may eventually go away because the Holy Spirit will not force Himself upon you. However, you may find your ability to hear from God diminishes and eventually you will not sense the leading to forgive. Then you get sick and ask God why you can't receive your healing. You have probably put that situation far out of your mind because you didn't want to think about it. Now you are sick and try to use your faith but nothing seems to work. I would call that a roadblock.

Now GOD DID NOT MAKE YOU SICK! He tried His best to help you and YOU IGNORED HIM. Now don't blame God and don't condemn yourself. Obedience is better than sacrifice. (I Samuel 15:22) Just make a U-Turn and obey the leading of the Holy Spirit. You can reverse the curse through obedience to God's Word and His leadings.

8. Staying in an Unhealthy Environment

When your spirit is sensitive and the environment around you is filled with ideas and behavior that are against what you believe and stand for, your spirit can rebel and your body can be caught in the middle of a tug of war. If the Holy Spirit is leading you to leave a job, city, or relationship and you know you should obey but are afraid to obey, your body may begin to break down under the stress.

If you have strong convictions, God can either lead you to speak up and take a stand or to leave. But the key is to listen to the Holy Spirit.

Be ye not unequally yoked together with unbelievers: for what fellowship hath righteousness with unrighteousness? and what communion hath light with darkness?
2 Corinthians 6:14

God may lead you to be bold and be a witness or God may lead you to slip away quietly. The most important thing is to be obedient to what God is leading you to do personally. If you develop the misconception that God has only one way for things to be dealt with, then you can be terribly misguided.

Our false beliefs and ideas can create a very unhealthy home life, work life, and relationships. These beliefs create patterns like a web we become caught in, adapt to, and consider it "normal." It may be normal for you, but if it leads to ill health then adjustments need to made if you want to be healed and live life more abundantly.

Those adjustments start with recognizing and changing your false beliefs. This could be something as small as a family belief that the mother always cooks, or the devastating idea that verbal and physical abuse are acceptable and expected. Changing the first idea may cause family discomfort (and the purchase of a cookbook), but changing the second could require removing yourself physically from the home.

A father who loves his family may desire to provide for them by taking a job that produces more money, but is a bad fit for him personally, and then suffer in his health. Is your job making you sick? Is it better to have more money or good health?

The mother who gets tired of cooking and feels unappreciated may develop migraine headaches or weakness (real or imagined) to escape what she does not want to do.

The person who is abused may want to escape, but out of fear stays put physically and escapes mentally and emotionally. Being disconnected physically by mentally escaping may be a temporary help, but often results in long term chronic pain, mental and emotional illness. This can allow the body to develop a final escape in a terminal illness.

Only you and the Holy Spirit know what is right for you. If you can find a way through the Word of God and the help of the Holy Spirit to live or work in a toxic environment and be a witness, then God has empowered you with grace to overcome! There is a time to stay and a time to go. Just don't get stuck in the idea of either staying or leaving. Jesus asked all of His disciples to "Follow Me." In other words, come be with me and go everywhere I go. They thought that they would be forever with Him in physical form. Things did not turn out as they had expected. His death was such a shock that it shook them to the core. They had dedicated their lives to a belief of Jesus setting up His kingdom NOW. Before He ascended, He told them to "Go forth." He said both "Come" and "Go" at different times for different reasons.

So God can change you, change your circumstances or ask you to remove yourself from the circumstances that are adverse to your health.

Staying in an unhealthy environment that is making you sick can have the same results as continuing to eat or drink something you know the Holy Spirit has asked you to stop. If you choose to continue subjecting yourself to what makes you ill, it is a choice which God has given you. There is no condemnation or judgement, but your health will suffer.

9. Trying to Act Beyond Your Faith

You may have heard a wonderful testimony of someone who was healed of the same thing that you are suffering in your body and be tempted to jump on the bandwagon of doing the same thing that person did, expecting the same results. You may also try to use a "formula" of faith that you heard someone else talk about. It's great to be inspired and get excited about the healing of others and the amazing blessings of healing and health. The truth is that you have seen the "results" of their faith and do not really know all they went through to get to that place. Faith is of the heart and who can see into the heart except God?

You may be encouraged and your faith stirred by a testimony, but true faith is based on God's testimony only—that is—His Word—what HE said. If you are standing on what someone else said, you are not standing on much. If you are standing on what God said, you are standing on the foundation of all existence, and God will not fall or fail.

Acting beyond your faith can mean the following things:

Acting solely on the word of others

Getting a little faith and taking a big step

Let's look at Peter because he had a little faith and took a really big step.

And when the disciples saw him walking on the sea, they were troubled, saying, It is a spirit; and they cried out for fear.

But straightway Jesus spake unto them, saying, Be of good cheer; it is I; be not afraid.

*And Peter answered him and said,
Lord, if it be thou, bid me come unto thee
on the water.*

*And he said, Come. And when Peter
was come down out of the ship, he walked
on the water, to go to Jesus.*

*But when he saw the wind boisterous,
he was afraid; and beginning to sink, he
cried, saying, Lord, save me.*

*And immediately Jesus stretched forth
his hand, and caught him, and said unto
him, O thou of little faith, wherefore didst
thou doubt?*

Matthew 14:26-31

Peter heard Jesus say, "Come," but
Peter was already in fear. He didn't know
if it truly was Jesus out there. In a state
of fear, he asked Jesus to prove who He
was. (Have you ever asked God to prove
Himself?) Peter had a little faith that
maybe it was Jesus, so giving Peter credit,
he stepped out of the boat and he did walk
on the water. But again, fear overtook him
and he *began* to sink. Now I have jumped

in a lot of water, swimming pools and lakes, and I never ever _began_ to sink. I just went straight down. Peter's faith wavered, it didn't leave him all at once.

If you have faith, you must have works or simply stated you must act on it. James 2:20 tells us that faith without works (or actions) is dead. But your actions must equally match your faith. If you have a little faith and a little confidence, you must take some action, but as my Dad said, "Don't go whole hog when half ready." Would you expect a second grader to take a college entrance exam? Go for what you are ready for and then progress.

Many people have tried to act beyond their faith. Faith comes, grows, and increases in strength as you read the Word and speak it out loud. This is necessary to get faith in your heart. When you try to take an action of faith and there is no faith in your heart, it can either be a discouraging disappointment or deadly.

An example of *disappointment* would be the person who had hands laid upon them in prayer for healing of their eyes and the need for eyeglasses. Being excited and then attempting to "force" healing to come, they refused to wear their glasses (or readers) to see the computer screen, read the newspaper, or worse—to drive. Well, if they are running into things, and reading with their nose 2 inches from the computer screen or paper, then the healing is not manifest. *Not wearing glasses* will not heal them, nor will it force healing to come. After doing this for a few days or weeks, there will be disappointment and inevitably be the question, "Why didn't I get healed?" A better idea would be to continually infuse yourself with the scriptures on health and healing until you could not wear your glasses because your eyes now focus properly.

Acting beyond your faith can be *deadly* when a believer refuses medical attention claiming to "stand on faith" when it becomes obvious that nothing has changed in the body physically. Death could be the result of inaction. I personally know of several people who could be alive today if they had not refused medical attention for treatable conditions. I honor their right to choose, but wonder if it would not have been better to still be alive providing for their families.

So how do you know just how much faith you have and how far you can go with your actions? Obviously, you can spend a lot longer time developing your faith for healing of nearsightedness (hopefully while wearing your glasses) than you can for a life threatening brain tumor.

Making an act of faith, any small act is important. Do something that is easy and simple at first. Then begin to do things that are not as easy and require more effort. If you have had a stroke, then move what parts you can. Stepping out in faith, you could write down and plan what you will do when health returns. If you play golf and have an injured back, you could polish your clubs or drive to the golf course. Your act of faith may be to stand and confess the Word daily over your body in front of the mirror. The point is, faith is of the heart. It is personal and only you and the Holy Spirit know what actions you should take and in what order. Healing is not forced from without. Let faith and health spring up from within.

10. Believing You Will Be Healed in the Future

By reading this book, I assume that you believe that God wants you well, that God is a good God and He sent His Son for deliverance from sin and sickness. If you have any doubts about that, then you must go back to the Bible and study the healing scriptures, because in order to be well you must believe upon the Lord Jesus Christ as your Savior and Healer.

I have contact with many believers strong in faith and I am always astounded at how many of them will request counseling and prayer to understand *"why God won't heal them."* For some reason it is easy to slip back into the thinking that God has to *do* something for us to be healed. That's like saying, "Why won't God save me from sin?" I seldom hear anyone say anything like that. We know Jesus has already died and shed His blood and saved the whole world full of sinners if they would only believe and accept Him.

It is done. It is finished. God already provided (past tense) healing and health for you. He doesn't have to *do* anything else. God has healed you. He has saved you. It was all in one package, healing and salvation...total restoration. Now you must take steps to get it into the physical body.

Change your language and change your thinking. Instead of thinking, "When God heals me I will _____," change it to, "When I am fully restored to health I will _____."

Rather than asking, "Why won't God heal me?" ask, "What is hindering me from *receiving* my healing?" It is a matter of receiving that you are struggling with. It is not a matter of talking God into healing, begging Him to heal, or bargaining with Him. He's already done it. It's deposited into your spiritual bank account. The question is, "When are you going to write a check on it and make a demand on what is already provided for you?"

According to God's spiritual law, you are not going to be healed sometime in the future; you are healed now. Let's review the basis of this spiritual covenant which I personally consider a legal document:

He is despised and rejected of men; a man of sorrows, and acquainted with grief: and we hid as it were our faces from him; he was despised, and we esteemed him not.

Surely he hath borne our griefs, and carried our sorrows: yet we did esteem him stricken, smitten of God, and afflicted.

But he was wounded for our transgressions, he was bruised for our iniquities: the chastisement of our peace was upon him; and with his stripes we are healed. Isaiah 53:3-5

This Old Testament scripture is a prophecy of the coming of the Messiah and the promise of what He will accomplish.

Peter quotes this as a finished work which we read in the New Testament:

Who his own self bare our sins in his own body on the tree, that we, being dead to sins, should live unto righteousness: by whose stripes ye were healed. I Peter 2:24

By His stripes you *were* healed.

Under the contract, there was a promise and Peter confirmed that it had been fulfilled. In order to get the spiritual into the physical, take the steps of meditating on these scriptures and speak them out loud in private until they get into your heart and mind and you develop strong faith. As you begin to become confident in your faith, the physical body will begin to change.

I pray that your eyes will be opened in understanding and your spirit quickened by the Spirit of God to any roadblocks that have prevented you from living in the abundant health Jesus Christ has provided for you!

Prayer Confession for Health
(repeat out loud)

Jesus bore my pains and carried my sickness and disease. He has redeemed me from the curse of the law, therefore there is no legal right, no legal claim for sickness, disease or pain to take hold in my body. The price has been paid.

***

I do not allow sin to take hold in my mind or my spirit, neither do I allow sickness to take hold of my body. I do not surround myself with evil images or listen to sinful discussions, nor do I surround myself with images of sickness and disease. I resist and shut out of my mind all talk and images of illness. I focus on the mighty redemption Jesus purchased for me—perfect health, perfect wholeness and deliverance from all evil.

***

You, Lord Jesus, have redeemed my life from destruction. The same Spirit that raised You from the dead quickens and makes alive every cell of my body. I am filled with the life of God. I am created from the minute particles of the totality of all that God is... and God is life. The atomic structure of my body vibrates with the energy of God. The light of that energy drives out all darkness, sickness, depression and pain. It cannot stay in my body which is filled with light.

***

My body is filled with life and because You defeated death, death has no power over me. Life reigns in every cell of my body and directs divine, robust health in all functions of this body.

***

I am everything God says I am and God says I am redeemed from the curse of sin, sickness and death, therefore my health has been restored and I receive all Jesus has done for me. I bless the Lord with all my soul for His redemption! I AM WELL!

BOOKS BY CHARLES CAPPS
AND ANNETTE CAPPS

Angels

God's Creative Power® for Finances

God's Creative Power® - Gift Edition
(Also available in Spanish)

BOOKS BY ANNETTE CAPPS

Quantum Faith®

*Reverse The Curse in
Your Body and Emotions*

Removing the Roadblocks to Health and Healing

Overcoming Persecution

BOOKS BY CHARLES CAPPS

New Release!!! Calling Things That Are Not

Triumph Over The Enemy

When Jesus Prays Through You

The Tongue – A Creative Force

Releasing the Ability of God Through Prayer

End Time Events

Your Spiritual Authority

Changing the Seen and Shaping The Unseen

Faith That Will Not Change

Faith and Confession

God's Creative Power® Will Work For You
(Also available in Spanish)

God's Creative Power® For Healing
(Also available in Spanish)

Success Motivation Through the Word

God's Image of You

Seedtime and Harvest
(Also available in Spanish)

The Thermostat of Hope
(Also available in Spanish)

The Tongue – A Creative Force – Gift Edition

How You Can Avoid Tragedy

Kicking Over Sacred Cows

The Substance of Things

The Light of Life in the Spirit of Man

Faith That Will Work For You

Annette Capps is an ordained minister, business-woman and licensed airplane pilot. A lifelong student of the Bible, her curiosity led her to investigate the similarities of "quantum physics" and the teachings of Jesus Christ. This powerful combination opened new dimensions  for those seeking a bridge between the Bible and modern science.

Building on her former teaching subjects such as *The Mind-Body Connection*, and *Changing the Course of Your Life*, she demonstrates the practical application of spiritual principles in everyday life.

Guest appearances on the Concepts of Faith television program with her father, author and teacher, Charles Capps generated extra-ordinary interest as have radio interviews and magazine articles. In addition to the book, *Quantum Faith®*, Annette has authored four other books entitled; *Reverse the Curse in Your Body and Emotions, Overcoming Persecution, Angels* and *God's Creative Power® for Finances*.

Annette and her husband reside in Tulsa, Oklahoma where she is the President of Capps Ministries which has locations in both Arkansas and Oklahoma.